Sam Is Six

by Katrina Davino • illustrated by Sarah Hoyle

Lucy Calkins and Michael Rae-Grant, Series Editors

LETTER-SOUND CORRESPONDENCES

m, t, a, n, s, ss, p, i, d, g, o, c, k, ck, r, u, h, b, e, f, ff, l, ll, zz, j, v, w, y, x

HIGH-FREQUENCY WORDS

is, like, see, the, no, so, has, his, of, says, go, to, for, look, me, he, you

Sam Is Six
Author: Katrina Davino
Series Editors: Lucy Calkins and Michael Rae-Grant

Heinemann
145 Maplewood Avenue, Suite 300
Portsmouth, NH 03801
www.heinemann.com

Cataloging-in-Publication data is on file with the Library of Congress.

ISBN-13: 978-0-325-13824-4

Design and Production: Dinardo Design LLC, Carole Berg, and Rebecca Anderson

Editors: Anna Cockerille and Jennifer McKenna

Illustrations: Sarah Hoyle

Photographs: p. 32 (pets) © Ermolaev Alexander/Shutterstock; inside back cover (socks) © AnEduard/Shutterstock; inside back cover (fox) © Kert/Shutterstock.

Manufacturing: Gerard Clancy

Printed in the United States of America on acid-free paper
3 4 5 6 7 8 9 10 MP 28 27 26 25 24 23
January 2023 printing / PO# 4500866727

Contents

Meet...

Sam   Dad   Mom

A Big Cake for a Big Kid

Sam is six,

so he will get a big cake.

Sam grabs the box
and adds in the cake mix.

He fills the pan
up to the tip-top.

The oven is hot,

so the cake can go in!

Tick tock, tick tock...

At last, Dad tests the cake
to see if it is set.

"Is it?" asks Sam.

"Yes!" says Dad.

2

Fox the Pup

Mom has a big box.

"It is for you, Sam!" Mom says.

Sam looks in the box.

He sees a dog with red fuzz!

It is not a big dog.

It is just a pup.

It sits up in the box
and begs for a snack.

Yip, yap, yip!

Mom hands Sam
a bit of hot dog.

The pup sits, so it gets a snack.

Sam hugs the pup.

It is so soft!

He looks at the tag,
and the tag says Fox.

Sam gets a big, wet kiss!
He grins and says,
"I like you, Fox!"

22

3

Can Mom Fix It?

Sam and Fox sit on the steps.

Fox picks up the doll and—ack!

The leg snaps off!

Sam grabs Fox,

and he grabs his doll.

He runs in to get Mom.

"Can you fix it?" asks Sam.

"Let's see...," Mom says.

Mom looks at the leg.

It is not so bad.

"I bet you can help me
fix it, Sam!" Mom says.

Mom digs in a box

and hands Sam a bit of wax.

Sam rubs wax on the leg.

Mom pops the leg back in and...

Did Mom and Sam fix the doll?
Yes!

PETS

Woof! Squeak! Meow! What's that sound? It could be a pet trying to talk to you. Pets can't use words the way people do, but they have their own ways of talking.

Have you ever heard a cat meow? Believe it or not, that cat is talking to you! Cats meow when they want our attention. Often a meow means "I'm hungry. Please feed me!" But meows aren't the only way that cats can talk. Has a cat ever rubbed against your leg? That means "Hooray! I'm so happy to see you!"

Have you ever heard a dog bark? Guess what? That dog is talking! When dogs bark, it can mean many things. Sometimes it means "Hey, look over there! Do you see that squirrel?" Other times it means "Please take me outside. I need to go pee!" Dogs talk in other ways too. Has a dog ever licked you? That means "I like you!"

Ask your reader some questions like...

- What happened in this book?
- Did Sam like his birthday present? How do you know?
- How did Sam's doll break? How did Sam and Mom fix it?
- Have you ever had something special break? What did you do?